PUB COLORING BOOK FOR ADULTS

CRYSTAL
COLORING BOOKS

ISBN-13: 978-1721960477
ISBN-10: 1721960473

THE FIGHTING COCK

The
Woolpack

The
Cat
Inn
The
Cat
Inn

NEW QUEEN

LOVERS REST

The Fox Inn

HAVEN
HOUSE
INN

CAT
+
FIDDLE

YEW TREE INN

NIGEL'S
INN

THE KINGS ARMS

RED SHOOT INN

Fritham
Inn

THE WOODEN SPOON

The Plough at Cadlder

The
Hare

THE PLOUGH

THE
FISH INN

WALKFORD

THE
ELM
TREE

ANCHOR INN

The
Salisbury
Inn

The
Kings

The
Ship

WALKFORD

THE
HOUSEMARTIN

THE WHI
RABBIT

THE NELSON TAVERN
LOCAL FAYRE

Queens Head

THE SHOE INN

COLOR TEST PAGE

COLOR TEST PAGE

www.ingramcontent.com/pod-product-compliance
Lightning Source LLC
Chambersburg PA
CBHW082008230526
45468CB00023B/2898
9781721960477